Beneath the Ice Fish Like Souls Look Alike

. . . .

BENEATH THE ICE FIS

IKE SOULS LOOK ALIKE

A POEM

emilia phillips

DURHAM, NORTH CAROLINA

BENEATH THE ICE FISH LIKE SOULS LOOK ALIKE

Copyright © 2015 by Emilia Phillips

. . . .

Published in the United States of America

Library of Congress Cataloging-in-Publication Data

Phillips, Emilia
Beneath the Ice Fish Like Souls Look Alike: a poem / by Emilia Phillips
p. cm.
ISBN-13: 978-1-4243-1803-2 (Paperback)

Cover composite by Philip McFee
Book design by Flying Hand Studio

Published by Bull City Press
1217 Odyssey Drive
Durham, NC 27713

http://bullcitypress.com

— for Gregory

The neighbors burn tires instead of cutting down trees.

A snake twists into an idling engine to warm.

An electrical current slithers through a child's finger into her arm.

(When the lights go out, you see the windows.)

. . . .

Where the band fell like a patrol, a tuba fills with snow.
When the facedown cheeks fill, they freeze like beets.

Tell the coroner's nephew cold

horns blow sharp. On an ear,

fleas wait on a dog to come round
for something to eat.

. . . .

A body adds and adds to a rock

        of calcium on the back of a hand.

     The dairy attracts stray cats.

A ring tightens on a finger in the cold morning.

       The dairy has no mice, the traps set rhetorically.

                 . . . .

Birds of the Republic

A crow's wing impaled on a weathervane.

A wren on a trombone slide.

A buzzard on a wooden swing.

A barn owl asleep in an upright tire.

. . . .

The trees sing like quarter rests.

The undertaker selects a tie to match the dead man's eyes.

A doe walks up the library's steps.

The letters of the word you want rise like fish to kiss your fingers.

. . . .

No children exist after midnight.

    The keyholes rest their eyes.

A green apple on the sill kneels to its rottenness.

            Snow angels like fallout hiss. . . .

                  . . . .

The mannequin crosses her arms by dropping them.

The leather boot remembers how to be skin.

The mannequin envies the photograph its light.

The boot remembers life as a dark heat inside.

. . . .

The city rises one story and cuts doors into windows.

The river once ran along the west of town; now it's frozen in the east. A bell still hangs on a door that opens to clay.

The old riverbed, now filled with beaters.

. . . .

A key scales the door to find

the lock. The water in the glass

    won't tip to meet

        the lips. A ship in the harbor dreams of

sinking. In the peephole

        blinks a pupil like a goat's.

        . . . .

Snow falls down the chimney of an abandoned house.

A candle in a drift melts its grasp.

The mannequin can't wear gloves, its fingers a rumor in its hands.

The metal chair shrinks further

into itself.

. . . .

The citizen speaks to the diplomat.

The motorcar powders its nose.

The diplomat responds in another
	tongue. The tires insist they can go
no further.

. . . .

The head of a cabbage opens under the faucet

    like love. Black mold

carpets the houses

    of the vale. Something old and something new trade

places. The bridge, evening blue,

    smiles in the gale.

    . . . .

Two Lincolns turn and turn but never face

one another. The chickens as if at feed peck

        at sleet. Pennies gleam in a bowl

of vinegar. A kettle without water

    cannot scream.

    . . . .

A baby grand's gutted to make a bed.

A cigarette's stubbed out in the barrel of a .38 held to a head.

A domino is on middle C reminds those who've forgotten how to play.

A moth in the starless day undresses

a mannequin.

. . . .

A snake coils in the empty toilet.

The moon is nothing but the moon.

The telephone rings once.

    The telephone rings twice.

. . . .

A chair knows the best diplomacy is form.

Ice understands form as expansion.

The metal chair in the abandoned house doesn't know it throws a shadow.

A plastic cup walks on four legs across the room.

· · · ·

A mouse eats the foam of a car seat.

       A cat tears the lining of a box spring.

The mouse dies in the vent.

       The cat births kittens under the bed.

                       . . . .

A glove needs to be reminded it is not a hand.

At the dairy, a machine pulls a dead cow's utters.

The archaeologist believes in projection over excavation.

(Inside the crematory, the fire shudders.)

. . . .

The diplomat debates

like heat. A horse flinches before

the lash lands on its rump. Heat moves

into cold

the way light moves into darkness. Children skate

to a raft frozen on the river but cannot

see its oarsman through the ice.

. . . .

The citizen takes a lover but is not a lover in return.

The ceilings of the neighbors' house are black. Nothing happens unless there's
music to accompany it.

The keys choir *heaven,*

heaven.

. . . .

A green bottle cannot contain brown liquid.

The archaeologist has never touched a spade.

At the dairy, a milk cow eats a poinsettia.

The archaeologist drinks warm cream and brandy for better

sleep.

. . . .

In the vacant chicken coop, a vagrant is sleeping.

The dog thinks all sounds come from the other side
of the door. The vagrant's breath through the wood slats freezes
into a horn. One day, the dog will run

its dog shape through a wall of snow.

. . . .

Where are the boots that fit the feet?

And the crowd that makes the street the street?

Where is the moon when there is no sun?

Here the troubadours turn a corner.

. . . .

The dog drops a candle at your feet like a bone.

The silent parade stops to admire their reflection in the windows.

A ship withdraws itself from the metaphor.

The danse macabre breaks an ankle.

. . . .

A child finds a tooth in the snow.

A cat spins in a dryer.

The child wonders if this is how his permanent
teeth will arrive.

The cat is found, its claws hooked in a blouse.

. . . .

In the abandoned

house, the floorboards crowd

like teeth. A cardinal flies in

through a broken

window and can't leave. The stones in the wall

moan against each other. The cardinal doesn't

know glass

of anything is made.

. . . .

The lights go out on one side of the street.

The vagrant drags a dead doe from the turnpike
down an alley. The sea leans into

the wind. The window
light breaks its frame.

. . . .

A cat walks up a suspension cable.

The metal chair offers a seat to the shadow.

The citizen knows his lover by his umbrella's angle.

The cat lands feet first on the water.

. . . .

The diplomat washes his hands in heavy cream

so they don't crack. The citizen keeps the tooth the brute
in the bar knocked out in cold milk until he gets

to the hospital. The archaeologist drinks
saltwater after kinesthetics.

A dog convinces a child to never speak again.

. . . .

A child on the stoop plucks feathers off a dead crow.

The archaeologist shoots a picture through the peephole.

A stone moves at the bottom of the river.

The hall exists as a series of doors exists as a series of paranoias.

. . . .

A moth flies in the mouth of a dead child.

The citizen ties a flamingo feather in his beard.

The band does an about-face

in the snow. A mother laughs instead of cries and shines

an apple on her coat.

. . . .

acknowledgments

. . . .

Thank you to Brittany Cavallaro, Ross White, and Bull City Press, who made these words rise to kiss the fingers; Gregory Kimbrell, whose poem-tales beget these gestures; and Amy Beeder, Keith Ekiss, and Lisa Russ Spaar, who were so kind to tip their hats to me from across a wide and busy street.

about the author

. . . .

EMILIA PHILLIPS is the author of *Signaletics* (University of Akron Press, 2013) and two chapbooks including *Bestiary of Gall* (Sundress Publications, 2013). Her poetry appears in *AGNI, The Kenyon Review, Narrative, Poetry*, and elsewhere. She is the recipient of the 2012 Poetry Prize from *The Journal*, 2nd Place in *Narrative*'s 2012 30 Below Contest, and fellowships from Bread Loaf Writers' Conference, U.S. Poets in Mexico, and Vermont Studio Center. She was the 2013–2014 Emerging Writer Lecturer at Gettysburg College, and serves as the prose editor for *32 Poems* and a staff member at the Sewanee Writers' Conference.